To: Amanda.
Thank you for
platform to

[?] — 16/2

C000053089

My Date With Depression

From Mental Uncertainty to Self-fulfillment

Kwame M.A. McPherson

Disclaimer

The information contained in this book is for general information purposes only. The information is provided by Kwame MA McPherson and while we endeavour to keep the information up to date and correct, we make no representations or warranties of any kind, expressed or implied, about the completeness, accuracy, reliability, suitability or availability with respect to this publication or the information, products, services, or related graphics contained in this publication for any purpose. Any reliance you place on such information is therefore strictly at your own risk. In no event will we be liable for any loss or damage including without limitation, indirect or consequential loss or damage, or any loss or damage whatsoever arising from loss of data or profits arising out of, or in connection with, the use of this publication.

Through this publication you are able to link to other resources and contacts which are not under the control of Kwame MA McPherson. We have no control over the nature, content and availability of those responsible for their management, operation or function. The inclusion of any links does not necessarily imply a recommendation or endorse the views expressed within them. At the time of writing, every effort was made to keep the information in this publication current. However, Kwame MA McPherson takes no responsibility for, and will not be liable for, information being out of date or unavailable due to technical or any other issue beyond our control.

Kwame MA McPherson can be contacted at www.kwamemcpherson.com

Check out the blog:
https://whywemendonttalk.blogspot.com

Copyright Year: February 2015, 1st edition; December, 2018, 2nd edition

Copyright Notice: Published by Kwame MA McPherson. All rights reserved. No part of this book may be reproduced in any form or by any means whatsoever, unless permission is granted by Kwame MA McPherson.
Results in this copyright notice:

© 2015 PKM Group © 2018 Kwame MA McPherson. All rights reserved

ISBN: 978-1-909389-26-7

Kwame MA McPherson

My Date With Depression

From Mental Uncertainty to Self-fulfillment

This book is dedicated to all those who are hurting and do not know it – a great, long life is still open to you

Dedication

To the Universe for this phenomenal journey, learning about myself and knowing what my purpose in life is;

To Our Ancestors, on whose shoulders I stand;

My family, the support and love is unmeasured and entirely and sincerely appreciated;

My close friends, who have been there every step of the way;

The beautiful people who have contributed to the man I am today, and to the one and only Queen who walks with me now.

CONTENTS

Check out my blog:

https://whywemendonttalk.blogspot.com

Acknowledgements

Father, Mother, Sisters and Brother, our journey has been as diverse as that of many other families but we still have each other regardless and not to forget my many nephews and nieces, too – everyone I love dearly;

Althea (Al) Grant, a fantastic speaker, earnest, genuine and wonderful human being and someone who I call my friend. Thank you for letting me work with you, meet and work with one of the world's greatest storytellers. That is etched in my memory for life.

Yvonne Hinds, my cousin, whose love and compassion helped me through a time when I didn't even know who I was or why I was here; young cousins, **Shaun** and **Jordan**, wonderful young men who helped shaped me, and my **Aunty Jean**, a one of a kind of elder;

Marcia Jackson and **Marcia Fenton**, beloved friends for life. Not to forget **McGuinne** and **Anna Ryan**, two of the most beautiful and loving people I know;

Janice Birthwright, thank you for so much;

Raymond Aaron, NY Times Best Selling Author of *Double Your Income Doing What You Love*, for the inspiration and the phenomenal 10-10-10 program enabling myself and co-partner, to complete this work in 10 weeks;

Althea Grant-Malcolm, editor extraordinaire; **Moya Thomas**, a great friend and having a wonderful perspective;

Travis 'Trey' Young, a true friend and African king, who inadvertently helped me 'find' this lost manuscript; **Malik Muhammed** and **Fitzroy Grant**, wonderful brothers and role models;

Pauline Clarke, a great friend who was around when this book was conceived and written under our now-defunct company brand - PKM Group - which provided the inspiring platform to help, publish and promote others;

Hilary (Abena) Barrett, Sister Dr Sandra Richards, Rasheda Ashanti and **Esther Austin**, words cannot express the love I have for you, your wisdom and spirit;

Primrose Granville, Joy Francis and **Paulette Harris-German**, the most beautiful people in the world.

And those many other brilliant people like Akua Saffron, Danette Gayle, Peaches Joy Williams (*A Daily Dose of Inspiration*), Keith Williams, Charlie English, Kathy Strachan, Charlene Fagan, Clara Brown, Garfield Lamont, Yvonne McKogg; my mentees such as Tamika Felina Pommells William (*Unearthing The Diamond*), Margaret Thorli (*Single Mother And The Dating Game*), Zoe Pennant (*The Scrabbled Mind*), Darren Ferguson (*How I Survived 5 Kidney Transplants And Won*), Evadney Campbell (*How To Carry Out Media Interviews*), Akeem T Gouldbourne (*Labeled An Immigrant*), Jacqueline

Hinds (*Journey to Empowerment*), Earl and Norma Morgan (*Against All Odds I'm Still Here*), I love you all just the same and with all of my heart. And to the many who I may have missed, I am sorry but you too have played a massive role in my life.

About the Author

An award winning author, Kwame is a prolific writer, Authorpreneur, poet, trainer, mentor and orator. In writing this book, he wished to share a pivotal time in his journey and the lessons he learnt. He loves helping others to share and enjoy his life experiences and aims to empower others in this way. He has a penchant for great chocolate, is a qualified football referee, certified trainer and mentor.

Book Shop window:

www.lulu.com/spotlight/baobabtreebooks

Website:

www.kwamemcpherson.com

Email:

kwame@kwamemcpherson.com,

kwamemamcpherson@gmail.com

Twitter:

@KwameMA

Facebook/LinkedIn:

Author Kwame McPherson

Instagram:

Kwame MA McPherson

Foreword

I would be more enthusiastic about a book that's breaking down stereotypical barriers for Black people and addressing their own mental health issues; someone, especially a man, being brave enough to accept that he has a problem, triumphantly works it out, then creates a successful life. Someone who's not just a survivor but a VICTOR!

This book, for me, is awesome because it sets out to celebrate a real man who tackled, alone, a real big problem and chose to write about his experiences. In so doing, saying to others, especially men, *'you're not weak because you fall but seek help to get back up ....'.*

This book is a page turner and a mind-set changer!

And, in an era when so much is shallow, I am privileged to know and call this man my friend. A man brave enough to admit he went through hell, yet is strong and caring enough to help others understand that they too can overcome.

Well done Kwame, for telling your story.

Althea Grant

Lawyer, International Professional Speaker, Les Brown protégée and successful *Les Brown in London* Events Promoter

Preface

This book was originally written in 2015 and for some reason was never birthed. As a matter of fact, I had lost it on a USB, only for my friend - Travis Young – to help me "find" it again. Now in 2018, it feels like this time was the right time. I am immensely proud of this part of my journey, opening up myself to talk about a time which was painful and emotional for me and also recognising that we as men, sometimes do not talk much about our struggles.

I think in order for me or us to heal, being able to share our deepest emotions, challenges or struggles, is something to celebrate and not be ashamed of. With that said, should this book assist just one man facing his own trials, then I will know I have fulfilled part of my purpose here on planet Earth.

Relevant Research

According to the Mental Health Org website[1], *people from black and minority ethnic groups living in the UK are: more likely to be diagnosed with mental health problems; more likely to be diagnosed and admitted to hospital; more likely to experience a poor outcome from treatment; more likely to disengage from mainstream mental health services, leading to social exclusion and a deterioration in their mental health.*

These differences may be explained by a number of factors, including poverty and racism and a legacy of the suffering pain and horror passed down from a recent history of Enslavement and Colonialism. That may probably be because mainstream mental health services often fail to understand or provide services that are acceptable and accessible to non-white British communities and

---

[1] *http://www.mentalhealth.org.uk/help-information/mental-health-a-z/b/bme-communities/*

16

meet their particular cultural and other needs. It is likely that mental health problems go unreported and untreated because people in some ethnic minority groups are reluctant to engage with mainstream health services.

African Caribbean people living in the UK have lower rates of common mental disorders than other ethnic groups but are more likely to be diagnosed with severe mental illness. African Caribbean people are three to five times more likely than any other group to be diagnosed and admitted to hospital for schizophrenia.

However, most of the research in this area has been based on service-use statistics. Some research suggests that the actual numbers of African Caribbean people with schizophrenia is much lower than originally thought.

African Caribbean people are also more likely to enter the mental health services via the courts or the police, rather than from primary care, which is the main route to treatment for most people. They are also more likely to be treated under a section of the Mental Health Act, are more likely to receive medication (rather than being offered verbal treatments such as psychotherapy) and are over-represented in high and medium secure units and prisons. This may be because they are reluctant to engage with services, and so, are much more ill when they do. It may also be that services use more coercive approaches to treatment with this sector of individuals.

The Mental Health Org www.mentalhealth.org

Introduction

In 2006, I journeyed through the darkest days of.my life. I had no idea how I got there, what it was I was going through or how to get out of it whilst I was in it. I had no idea how to acknowledge my emotional, physical, mental or spiritual failing state. I could not shout or scream for help or speak about the place I was in since I was never taught how to do so. Naturally, the manifestation became evident in how I treated myself, doing things I wouldn't normally do and treating others how I would never consider doing at any other rational time. My entire character altered from who I was to who I never thought I could be.

Yet, it was during that time I grew mentally, emotionally and spiritually, coming to understand, accept and embrace a time which was vital in my journey, development and way to BE. As much as I made the effort to turn myself around, I didn't do it alone. There was help; lots of it from family, exes, girlfriends and a wonderful counsellor. So, some eight years later, I decided to write about my experience as a Black man and the challenge I faced when I felt and thought life and everything else was against and killing me.

This book is not designed to be complex or present solutions garnered from a psychologist's 'lay-on-a-couch' examination or solution. This book is NOT suited for everyone since each person's state will be different and some may even be medically diagnosed. I have tried to keep this book simple since the solutions can be for many people as they were for me.

Within this book you will find very simple exercises at the end of some chapters that, I hope, will enable you to make sense of where you're at and how you got there. They have been designed in a way that allows you to take small but easy steps which are by no means a fast-track way to health and ultimately holistic wealth. **This book is just my way of helping you to be the greatest person you are here to be. It took me a while to get out of my**

own way but finally when I had, I became a better me – you can be GREATER you too.

Kwame MA McPherson
http://whywemendonttalk.blogspot.com
www.kwamemcpherson.com

What Stops Men from Asking for Help?

Professor Dinesh Bhugra[2] states social expectations about masculinity, particularly the view that men will be able to cope as they are perceived to be stronger, may contribute to a perception that it is unmanly to seek help. The way boys are brought up not to cry means that men may find it extremely difficult to express their feelings to anyone, including their male friends. Such a phenomenon is even more common in certain cultures.

Geert Hofstede, a Dutch sociologist, posited that cultures have five dimensions, one of which is related to masculinity/femininity. These attributes are related to learned styles of inter-personal interactions. Masculine cultures suggest that boys do not cry and should fight back and prevail in performance games. Competitive sports are part of the school curriculum and macho behaviour in the

---

[2] Professor Dinesh Bhugra, *The Truth About Men and Depression: Suffering in silence means more suffering, says the president of the World Psychiatric Association,* http://www.spectator.co.uk/health/features-health/9370552/the-truth-about-men-and-depression/, 22 November 2014

workplace is expected. In cultures with a high masculinity index, the engine power of their cars is important to men and they live in order to work. In such highly masculine societies the fate of the poor is seen as the poor's problem, thus any failure to achieve is personal rather than systemic. Men become more attractive to women by their achievement and status. Among the masculine cultures are Japan, German-speaking countries, Latin American countries and English-speaking countries such as the US, UK, Australia, New Zealand and Ireland.

These cultures encourage men to be macho and in control of everything including their emotions. They may therefore find it difficult to express some emotions in particular those of sadness, tearfulness and depression as 'men don't cry'. This means that a lot of these feelings get internalised, making it difficult to seek help. Men also tend to use more macho and violent methods of suicide such as hanging, guns or jumping from heights. Often feeling low is accompanied by tiredness and variations in mood as the day progresses, sadness, tearfulness, sleep disturbances and altered sleep patterns, low libido, poor appetite and loss of weight.

Depression in men can often present with irritability, outbursts of sudden anger, increased loss of control, risk-taking, aggression and increased alcohol intake to mask feelings of depression and irritability. Men may also use drugs more often to self-medicate and hide feelings of depression, as the general stereotype is that men do not get depressed and if they do, it is 'moral weakness'. Therefore, men tend to cope with and manage underlying depression in different ways. Often men are competitive and depression is interpreted as a sign of failure and therefore they may find it difficult to share these feelings with anyone. They may feel isolated but may not acknowledge that. In addition, their internal world would emphasise their feeling a failure and bleak views of the world and their future. Studies have shown that between 60 and 90 per cent of those who commit suicide have mental disorders. Thus early diagnosis and management is critical.

Black Men in Particular

Althea Grant, lawyer, human rights lobbyist and advocate breaks down the complex issue Black men face by stating, *"It's not because they, Black men, are more prone but rather that the system is racist and afraid of African/Caribbean people therefore the high incidence of actual mental health difficulties is but an indication of the systemic racism that punishes Black people far more strenuously than other peoples."*

You may be wondering how my journey towards **'My Date with Depression'** began? Like you, it began uneventful enough and it was not until I was heading for deep waters that it dawned on me as where this part of my life's journey was being diverted to. As with anything, sometimes the best way to explain a voyage was to go carefully over the map and retrace the steps from the beginning…

The Explorer in Me

In 2003, I migrated to Canada. A couple of years prior, I had visited the country, immediately falling in love with the place. There were several reasons for my 'falling in love' but for now I leave that right there since what eventually ended up getting my long-term attention was Canada's support for small business and entrepreneurs, the high standard of living, beautiful green spaces and the pristine cleanliness of the place; not to forget the wholehearted friendliness of the Canadian people. The romance and my rose-tinted glasses quickly darkening, spiralling downwards when that illusion was swiftly shattered. I found out that they, the people, were no different to the British and their isms. Yet, even so, it was so Toronto was massively different from London, with its consistently wet and grey weather, cramped environment, small homes, narrow and dirty streets and lower standard of living. Toronto and its environs was a modern metropolis, in every sense of the word. I understood what the term "New World" meant.

I had happily declared to myself that I could "see me living here"... you know, settling down, getting away from the single life, having a family, and enjoying the rewards of my labour since everything within the country was geared for and to the family. But, looking forward to settling down and that long-term companionship and commitment came with its numerous experiences and "fun" times with the opposite sex, which I would not deny.... Yet within those fun times, I was unconsciously searching for the "one", someone to fill my empty vessel and make me whole. Someone who would "fix" me.

So Canada offered an integrated society designed for the family; regardless of the weather – spring, summer, fall or winter – some activity would be taking place and could be had for the entire family to enjoy. Some indoor stuff in the winter, when it was too damn cold to even go outside (not that it stopped the hardened souls but I just did not see me skiing or ice skating over ice or freshly fallen snow) or summer stuff when the hot days lasted for those summer months - Caribana and Soccerfest plus the multitude of barbeques, great ways to enjoy the scorching ball of fire in the sky.

Canada had great summers in comparison to London, where one could be 'lucky' for a good, solid week of hot sun. I truly struggled to deal with the Canadian winters since I had never before experienced such cold. Not then, not since. Imagine temperatures where it was -7c but a wind chill rendered it to -40c. Yes **-40c!** Or where a weatherman differentiated between simple snow falling, which was heavy at the best of times and when a blizzard was on the way; so one was cooped up in their home like a frozen bird unable to fly. *Trust me, freezing did not cut it since even London was not that cold at its most dreary! Now, why had I decided to leave London? What drove me to Canada? Looking back, I must have been crazy but I seriously have nothing but admiration and love for* *those Jamaicans who were able to manage the transition. Massive respect.*

I grew up in the ever vibrant city of Kingston, Jamaica, though I was actually born in the UK. Reverse migration one might say. Yet, I ended up home (with my father and brother) due to the dysfunction within my own family. But as a young man and in the mid-80s, I decided upon returning to London, to a country I had no recollection of or knew. Even though it was the place of my birth, everything was as foreign to me as I was to it. I tried to make the best of it but, I never actually 'fit in' try as I might. That indefinable "something" was always blocking my progress and I unable to put my finger on it, even though, I had a semblance of success. After all, I had acquired all that could be acquired by an upwardly mobile African-Caribbean man, like, going to college, university, having the "good" job, home, making my own way and so on. It was later, when it dawned on me about how the United Kingdom really was and my place within it. Funnily, **I still was 'unsettled' even after** attaining the many qualifications; at one stage, I was even called 'Professor', by footballing peers! I was kept busy by what I was ingrained to believe by others and society per se, distracting me rather than allowing me the space or time to face the source of my unsettled feelings.

My first ever job was in a 24-hour convenience store (they no longer exist in the UK) and it was my baptism into racism and how it reared its head in subtle ways. I remember being called 'boy' a number of times by the store manager and one day I told him, in no uncertain terms that slavery ended over two hundred years ago and I did not take kindly to being addressed in that way. If I recall rightly, I had a metal napkin holder in my hand at the time as I had been cleaning it, ready to use it. Suffice to say, he never called me boy again. As I continued to assimilate, I acquired what some would call respectable jobs in the Civil Service, Local Authority, Housing Association, Charity and Voluntary organisations; it felt like I must have traversed every public sector organisation there was but still itched for something more. Something to anchor me, make me feel as if I could finally call the place home.

Moving to Canada seemed the right choice but to tell you the truth my heart was always set on Jamaica, where I would travel virtually every year since immigrating in the 80s. Two years being the longest time I had ever been away but ultimately, Canada had called me to her and unbeknown to me, this was where my walk in the wilderness had truly begun.

List a time when you ever had a good or bad experience? What did that feel like? How did you deal with it?

1.

2.

3.

4.

5.

6.

7.

The Truth: *what causes depression*?

Typically, there were several causes for depression:

- Job loss,

- Childhood trauma,

- Financial woes,

- Failed relationships,

- Death of loved ones,

- Heredity,

- Relationship difficulties,

- Separation and divorce,

- Stressful jobs and lack of support at work or at home,

- Not being promoted or being promoted above one's capabilities,

- Becoming a new father.

For men, the supposed breadwinners or heads of the household and for example: losing a job, having no money or even a redundancy, could be seen as making them impotent, which once compounded by feelings of rejection and low self-esteem, could lead to feelings of depression. The realisation of the reasons for my own experience came later.

Do any of the mentioned causes of depression resonate with your experience?

YES   NO

How would YOU describe the scenario of how it came about and who was involved?

Life Sucks!

Professor Dinesh Bhugra in his article The Truth About Men and Depression wrote, *there are differences related to cultures and countries, but men are*

Figure 1 Google: Labelled for Reuse

more likely to complete the act of suicide whereas women are more likely to attempt suicide. As a result of the British legacy in many countries in the Commonwealth, the act of suicide remains illegal, so if your gun does not get you, the legal system will. More than 40 years ago, looking at low rates of suicide in black men in New York, it was observed that the rates of suicide were indeed low but those of homicide in this group were high, indicating that men swaggered their way out by arguing, 'I will kill or get killed.' Men tend to use more violent methods in completing suicide, and they tend to deal with their depression by drinking or through aggression or acts of violence[3].

African Caribbean men were unique. Our his-story making us who we were today and what we went through now, could be traced to the massive trauma our ancestors endured. Women too have been devastated by the **Maafa** (*see definition at the end of this chapter*), the both of us, a testimony to that legacy. Our latent, negative behaviours manifesting themselves in how we reacted or responded in particular situations. Some would argue against such a finding but I myself have an open mind since I know how I previously behaved.

So What Happened?

There were many incidents' or signs, long before everything unravelled in Canada. Instances in which I behaved as if I was unaccountable to everyone and anyone, living as if my purpose was

---

[3] Professor Dinesh Bhugra, *The Truth About Men and Depression: Suffering in silence means more suffering, says the president of the World Psychiatric Association,*http://www.spectator.co.uk/health/features-health/9370552/the-truth-about-men-and-depression/, 22 November 2014

strictly to accumulate riches, not to disseminate or share my life purpose which I did not even know. The funny thing was... Truth always revealed itself, catching up with the unaware me, and at times I least expected. *This TRUTH pushed me into the uncomfortable limelight of embarrassment and shame.*

There I was, in my new home called Canada, Brampton, Greater Toronto Area or GTA - to be exact - and aside from the reason for migrating, there was another

Figure 2 Google: Labeled for Reuse

one.

I had partnered with two friends who also had the dream of living and working in Canada, so we set about building a company as soon as we landed and since I would be the first to migrate, it was my responsibility to lay the groundwork and start the ball rolling until they arrived. There I was newly arrived and excited to be in Canada and in my enthusiasm began to build the business. It was to be in telecommunications. At the time the cell/mobile phone market was just evolving and UK and Europe were at the forefront of this new technology. North America, and Canada, in particular, were still lagging behind. We saw an opportunity and figured we would import cell/mobile phones into an entirely new market. Unfortunately, and pretty soon, things began to unravel.

One of the things I loved about Canada, at the time, was the support for small business and entrepreneurs and this translated into the provision of financing. As a new arrival I was able to obtain lines of credit I could only dream of in the UK. Going to Canada also introduced me to personal development.

Figure 3 Google: Labeled for Reuse

Though I knew of the concept, it never truly dawned on me until I was in my new home. I met the phenomenal motivational speaker, T Harv Eker, author of *Secrets of a Millionaire Mind*™, when I attended his very first Millionaire Mind Intensive event in Toronto. The seminar moved me in such a way I had never experienced before, exposing my emotional state, money blueprint and relationship with myself. Everything was revealed to me in all its ugliness and entirety and I became excited and decided to spring into action from what I had learnt. What I did not have though was the knowledge of how to do so! My enthusiasm was fine but without the required knowledge I was already off to a bad entrepreneurial start. So, of course, after leaving those three intense days, I came away with a new self-belief of just wanting to make things speedily happen and so I applied and got lines of credit and just went crazy. Thousands of dollars I might add!

I invested in businesses and purchased property without the financial wherewithal or knowledge as taught by the greats: Marcus Mosiah Garvey[4], Napoleon Hill[5], Robert Kiyosaki[6] or Tony

Robbins[7]. I was like a child seeing the beautiful blue and warm Caribbean Sea for the first time, diving straight in without the thought of whether I would swim or sink. To say I nearly drowned was an understatement. There I was without any floatation devices, paddling like a new born, going nowhere fast and lo and behold, began to descend.

There was a new business partner I had joined with and he proved to be unreliable and incapable; not his fault, just the way he was. Eventually and naturally, everything crashed. But within the muck and completely opposite, there was one other partner, the greatest human being I now call a dear friend. We purchased property together and as a result of my own deals going sour, it dragged him down with me. My impact, affecting his credit. To this day he's the greatest, humblest of individuals I know and his wife was just as superb. Perfect people.

---

[4] Garvey, Marcus (1923) *The Philosophy & Opinions of Marcus Garvey*; Garvey, Marcus (1986) (edited by Tony Warner) *Message to the People: the course of African Philosophy*
[5] Think and Grow Rich™
[6] Rich Dad, Poor Dad™
[7] Ultimate Power™

Beautiful souls. Then there was one other different person who I met through a networking event and together, we invested in a principle property. Eventually though, his true colours came through and he worked it in a way for his family to move in, when at the time it was supposed to have been only temporary. Looking back, I do blame him for the deceit, yet take responsibility for my own deficient decision making. The specific lessons I learnt from these particular episodes were published in my book, *7-Tips for the Virgin Entrepreneur: doing it for the first time* and in it I detailed how to select solid partners. Every act, every decision to partner with people without due reference or diligence caused me to end up in a place I never thought I would be.

What made matters worse was that I had rekindled my relationship with an ex and she came to visit me in the middle of everything and her presence brought out more of my insecurities. So not only had the seminar identified my money management deficiencies, having her in my space brought out deep-seated, underlying, generational emotional baggage or what had been inherited from before. This burden, a residue of the traumatic relationship between my parents, when I - a five or six-year-old child - witnessed the violence and abuse my father inflicted upon my mother. The images as real as if I was the star in the unheard of movie.

So my journey saw me moving from one extreme to the next; my behaviour floundering. I would 'hide' as I built and collapsed businesses, earnt trust yet destroyed relationships, living as if everything was great yet be in denial. So, from one extreme to another - I was living a lie.

Maafa: *is a Kiswahili term for disaster, calamity or terrible occurrence. This term has been used to describe the Trans-Atlantic Slave Trade/Middle Passage. people of African Descent are invited in an attempt to honour our ancestors who have suffered through the middle passage AND the lives that continue to be compromised due to racism and oppression.* **Source:** *www.maafasfbayarea.com*

Can you recall the times when *you* selected the 'wrong' people?

Wading Through the Wilderness

Figure 4 Google: Labeled for Reuse

I was scared. The impact of watching my fledgling empire crumble about me was hard to take. The business went under. My property disappeared. What made it worse was that I could not face the other people who had believed in *me* and invested in *me*. The calls began and I chose to hide from all and sundry, refusing to take them. You know the ones from creditors and the trusted partners I brought into one business. I felt like there was absolutely nothing I could possibly do and with no answers, huge debt and a failing relationship hanging over my head; I was speeding to oblivion.

Even that great friend and partner went out on a limb for me, putting his family and livelihood at risk because of his belief in me - that was hard to take. Worse, I started to internalise my fear as it seemed nothing would or could alleviate my situation and I

45

tried hiding my predicament by staying silent, failing to communicate my pain to anybody.

When my ex came to visit, we went to Niagara Falls for a weekend. Along the way and with her being with me, my fear materialised in what I was going through and effecting everything I did, from money management to the inability to emotionally open up, hold her hand or even to kiss her. And still I never made the time or created the space to assess my situation, so things just went from bad to worse and stress became an unseen companion. There she was with me in Canada and I was sincerely glad to see her, believe me but it was a hollow joy. We spent a wonderful time together as couples in love in any good relationship but I had emotionally evaporated, being mentally mauled, physically pained and financially failing, all of which played out in incident after incident.

I once went and visited an herbalist (who also later became a good friend) and she gave me a cleansing bath. While on the massage table, kneading out the stress aches in my body, she said she saw something in me that disturbed her. What she said frightened me even more, she said she was watching me die right before her eyes, not literally but, in essence, my spirit was. And on that massage table, right before her, my life-force was draining away, being sucked from my physicality like juice from a plum, the skin shrivelled until it was old, wrinkled and without life. A light slowly being extinguished.

After that revelation, I was even more fearful of living and being alive.

Niagara Falls

So there I was driving with my girlfriend to Niagara, to visit the falls but once again I tried 'hiding' my feelings,

Figure 6 Google: Labeled for Reuse

this time from something so mundane, I even have trouble remembering what it was but what I do recall was the tongue lashing I received on the ride from Toronto. You see, I had a tendency to avoid confrontation, unwilling to deal with those tough issues, having the discussions. I would choose to run away rather like when I watched, hiding underneath the kitchen table, as my father and mother fought each other; my father raining licks, my mother giving as best as she could.

Now, if you know how long the drive from Toronto to Ontario was, you would know what we endured, listening to her home truths and realising they were entirely my responsibility. No shirking but wishing for the miles to disappear. She had been right and needless to say, there was no lovemaking at Niagara when we were there. On reflection too, I was afraid of being assertive, a remnant of watching my parents and me thinking how I was supposed to be.

And yet, after we strolled through the town of Niagara Falls, stopping and having fun in the amusement arcades, we would have a most uplifting moment. It happened by the actual Falls, itself. We stood by the guardrail, watching white water roar and spectacularly flow over the river's lip and into a massive foaming pool. The water's drizzle wet us both on the sightseeing overhang. Then, just as suddenly as we stood watching the Niagara River turn into the Falls, I felt something and whatever it was, it put everything into perspective. It seemed like an invisible power had surged from the Falls in such a way I never felt before (until I later got to Africa, of course) overcoming and overpowering me. This omnipresent might shot through me, making me aware of the glory and magnificence this world had to offer and *how* petty everything I thought I was going through actually seemed. Turning to the heavens I cried and gave thanks for the experience and standing on that rim, I sobbed and cried right there on her shoulder, asking for her forgiveness. Emotionally I was a wreck, unable to say to the woman whom I said I loved why I was behaving the way I was. Why my money mismanagement was a demonstration of how disconnected I was from me. I was not in touch with my feelings or knew how to convey them. How I wore the proverbial mask and found it hard to open up about my physical, mental, emotional and spiritual pain, clamming up tighter than a sea clam, trying to find the answers from my own limited mind and know-how. Coming away, this was where my true struggles began.

Eventually she returned to the UK and I became even more sick, but from that experience, my inner-eye was prised open and from then on as more experiences came my way, the signs continued to reveal themselves but I kept fumbling like a blind man feeling his way along a darkened corridor, searching for answers, seeking to latch on to anything that resembled my salvation. And that was how I ended up in church.

Africa Calling

In December of 2006, we visited Africa for the first time in my life and many for her, I would always be extremely grateful to her, for exposing me to the land of our ancestors. I had never been to the

50

Motherland and in particular, Ghana, which blew me away. Outside of Jamaica, it felt like home.

Figure 8 Google: Labeled for Reuse

And still, even while there, I was struggling with myself and episode after episode. In one instance, on the flight over, she was sleeping and the flight attendant passed by offering to retrieve drinks she had given us earlier. When she asked the question whether my ex had finished I said she had when she had not. When my ex awoke, instead of saying what was, I said the flight attendant had taken her drink. Would you know the way truth works, my ex asked the flight attendant why she took her drink, only for the attendant to say I was the one who said she had finished. Right then, if I could have jumped from the plane without a parachute, I would have and for something so simple and stupid. Once again, I was in that space of concealment and from what, I was still yet to find out.

The plane landed and the first thing I did was kiss the hallowed ground, my way of showing respect by offering libation of sorts, to those who had made the tortuous journey and I, as their descendant, was finally returning home. As we gathered our bags and walked through the terminal I shed a tear. I was praying and hoping that being in the Motherland would help me find myself.

Yet, even in Africa, there were times when my negative-self showed up like bleached white clothes hung out to dry but I felt within me something was shifting. It was as if I was shedding an old skin to reveal something underneath, ugly or pretty, I had no clue. What I came to realise, though, was that being in the Motherland had put my entire life under a microscope moreso than when we were at Niagara Falls, every minute bit of my life and when it was compared to what our ancestors had experienced, my troubles were put into nothing. Everything about them was raped away whereas I had a choice - I could wallow in self-pity or pull myself up.

One of our first trips was to the Cape Coast enslavement fort, a whitewashed building on the Ghanaian coastline with parapets that overlooked the beach and town. Our guide told us that from the parapets we would see in the distance, the crucifix spires of three churches. And for sure when we ventured to the top of the fort and looked over the town, we saw the churches and their spires, clearly against the bright, blue sky along with the hundreds of people living within the city. Within myself I found it ironic that those who professed to follow the Christ and supposedly loved their fellowman, allowed a cruel crime of humongous proportions to take place right in their view. Or better yet under their noses. What did that say about them and their "religion"? I was extremely puzzled.

We climbed down steps and made our way into the dungeon below the fort and there I experienced another phenomenal spiritual moment that has stayed with me to this day. It was dark and foreboding with a single bulb hanging from a wire, its light bouncing from the walls and the rocky roof, causing shadows to flit against the craggy walls. The atmosphere was stifling and I felt I had been bundled in with another few hundred people, many whom I never knew, into a room made for many less than that number. I felt the spirits calling me and I was without a doubt affected by their presence, their deafening silence embracing me. I was sure that there was an effect on the others too since most of us, when we remerged into the beautiful daylight, were crying.

Once in the dungeon, our tour guide showed us a rough line running parallel to the floor. He then showed us a window slit, no bigger than one-foot-high and about half that wide, high up on the uneven wall. Naturally, within the dungeon, daylight could barely be seen. He then explained that because the land on the outside was level with the bottom of the slit, anytime rain fell the water made its way into the cell. Imagine. Hundreds of people. Packed in a space made for much less than that. Faeces. Urine. Rainwater. Grime. All swilling underfoot, knee-high or waist-high, even shoulder-high. And this, in a confined, heat-suffocating place. I cried.

We made our way out to the ground floor. Nothing needed to be said by any of us. Once there, we stood by the dungeon entrance and right beside it, was another large, wooden door. A huge padlock secured it. I was curious and decided to force it ajar as far as I was able to. I was dumbstruck. A stench assaulted my nose *that* would stay with me forever and I still remain, to this day, unable to describe. When I asked the guide why the room was locked, he said that they, the caretakers or custodians of the fort, were unable to get it clean. That's right. **They were incapable of getting it cleaned.** I was silenced. Here was a room which after hundreds of years, was still unable to be scrubbed. I repeat. *Imagine...after hundreds of years, there was still a room that they were unable to scour of the blood, tears, perspiration, excrement, effluent and death, to the time when we visited in 2006.*

The visit to Cape Coast had a profound effect on me. It changed my outlook on my life, prompting me to appreciate the simple things, giving gratitude to those who went before. The story even continued when I had another spiritual encounter on Labadi Beach.

It was a wonderful warm evening and we had decided to go and chill on the beach. We made and sat around an open fire, by snapping and using dry twigs, branches, old newspapers and a lighter to ignite the fire. It was dark. A starry night. The constellations as bright as if a billion people were shining their own torch. For a while, we quietly sat listening to the sea as it stroked the sand, a rhythmic pattern that sounded soothing and melodic, completely creating a truly spiritual vibe. It was as if the spirits of our ancestors were swimming in the surf. I took a walk along the sand and to the water's edge, where it ebbed and flowed. I stood with the water at my ankles as it splashed ashore, uttering a prayer, thanking my ancestors for their sacrifice and looking towards the heavens in reverence, for their and my journey. But what happened next scared and yet reassured me. Suddenly, as soon as my prayer was finished the ocean went out and as it immediately rushed back in, it reached my knees as it moved towards the shore. Standing on that beach, I knew someone, somewhere or something had heard my prayers.

Finding Salvation?

On my return to Canada my trials continued. My girlfriend had returned to the UK and my mental and emotional state floundered unabated. The conflict within me deepening. The fight between knowing who I truly was against what I had been bought up to believe - waging their own emotional battle.

And so, I was invited to church by the friend who offered me the herbal bath. An ardent churchgoer, I allowed her to influence me that a solution to my deep-seated issues could only

Figure 10 Google: Labeled for Reuse

57

be *fixed* within the church and I went, the name of which I have long forgotten. For a while, it was a place where I thought the answers to my problems would be revealed. Naturally, I became a church member, singing all the songs, attending and associating myself with other members to the point where they had my phone number and would call me to let me know about some church activity or the other. But my behaviour became erratic and I became more withdrawn and even more introverted, isolating myself from and around my family, those closest to me. Everything about and around the church became my *new* focus and nothing else mattered but being in my cousin's basement apartment, blinds drawn, room in darkness and then being within four walls to talking about a book of books and its most revered individual with its thousand-year-old stories, some of which themselves were uplifted from texts written centuries before. I was in a war between what I knew about my own story and the one which others had imposed upon me and million others. With this on top of everything else, I fell further into a bottomless pit.

My cousin knew this was not me but naturally, I would not have known that as I sank further into a world where nothing else mattered but being locked away, going for long, lonesome walks and talking to myself, then finding some temporary reprieve in church. It was abnormal behaviour and it came to a head one day, when I returned to her home and told her I got baptised.

Getting Baptised

Figure 12 Google: Labeled for Reuse

I was unemployed, with no income to even begin to pay off the debt. The hounding and harassment continued, I just could not see a way out so I reverted to what was comfortable by pursuing 'divine' intervention. One day, while sitting in the pew, listening to the preacher preach about sins and sinners, he called those who wished to repent to the front of the packed congregation and there I was – front and centre. I had decided to 'banish' my sins away for a higher way of being. Yet, while I stood in front of the pulpit that day, I noticed the stained window stretching above the dais, almost reaching the ceiling, with every single image I saw there was a *white* Christ in some form or another and even that had not jolted me into recognising everything for what it was. Unaware and unbeknownst to me at my most vulnerable, I had been duped and later that evening I returned to be baptised and baptised I was. The water washed over me dressed in my white robe as the pastor held me under for a few seconds before I re-emerged. And t, to tell you the truth over time I realised that was all it was - a symbolic exercise. And it seemed as if divine intervention had not worked since my turmoil and angst continued.

Continued Conflict

Being baptised had not stopped my struggles and things only got worse. I became more isolated and clung to the church as the battle raged within me, especially after being aware of my ancestors' true story. I felt that religion, whether Christianity or any other, played a massive role in enslaving them and it was harder to balance and digest its involvement in my life and my efforts in seeking so-called 'salvation'. Slavers used Christianity as a way of subduing the spirit of African people and for me and for that reason, I recognised that my impending enlightenment was not aligned with any church or its teachings. My ancestors *had* laid the foundation and I eventually found that salvation started from within me.

The answer seemed elusive like a cat chasing a dark spot on a blank white wall. After losing everything I had ever dreamt of, including the goal of becoming a true, fully fledged entrepreneur, I felt like an abject failure and knew I needed to find employment and that was hard to do. After all, I had made a commitment to be all I knew I could be but here I was falling at the first hurdle but then…my cousin entered the frame and for that I love her for life. She was witnessing my uncommon behaviour and gradual downfall and was the one who spoke to me in no uncertain terms. One day she just asked me a few questions...*Who are you? What are you doing and why? When you first came to Canada you were not like this. What happened?* It was enough for me to ponder and something snapped within me. I began to turn my life around. I asked questions...

Who are YOU?

What are YOU doing and why?

Who brought YOU here?

Learning to Love Life, Every Day

I may have moved on from feeling sorry for myself, the businesses and money I lost and the hurt I caused to myself and others but my trials did not end there since it seemed my road to 'recovery' had only just begun. It was while in another relationship that my 'stuff' continued to reveal itself. This time though, I was able to recognise it for what it was and deal with it in the way I thought best - which was to walk away from a woman I said I loved. Another decision that was hard to swallow.

One More Life-Changing Trial

I thought that over the months and years I had made the time to work on myself, by reading the right books and attending the correct personal development seminars; hoping this would help me to recognise the behaviours. Yet all I was doing was plastering over the scars and failing to deal with the source of my behaviours. Maybe that was my arrogance. Being Mister-Know-It-All. Maybe I had felt I was "healed" after attending a few self-development seminars.

Everything converged when I chose to run, again, from a simple discussion. My childhood past exposing itself in all its glory. The truth unable to stay hidden. During the discussion, I realised I was playing out what I thought I had dealt with after all my self-development remodelling. Armed with this knowledge, I asked for help. I asked her for the support I needed to overcome the shadow which had prevailed throughout my life until then. I told her I needed counselling. Being the fantastic woman she was, she referred me to one.

Looking back, the relationship ended between us as I said I needed time to 'fix' the challenges I was facing but on my return, she had moved on. But that decision took me to where I was today, making me a much better man because of and especially her. I would not lie, now and again I have pangs of regret because I truly loved this woman and knew...she loved me too. Yet, I needed to take action, find out what was causing my 'pain', I needed to deal with myself once and for all. I needed to acknowledge and realise that in life, beautiful people helped us on our road to be. But, that was life. Some people came into our lives guiding us to be a better version of ourselves.

During my counselling session, I received a 'golden nugget' from the counsellor and it went off like an explosion in my head and because of it, my life completely changed. In our session, she asked questions and I always felt that my own deficiency was down to the fact that I never grew with my mother. But when she said I was wrong and that I was modelling myself on my father – I was completely floored! All along I thought that in my formative years because there had been an absence of feminine energy within our home, this was the reason why I kept 'running' away. It was because of what I had seen and experienced and grew with my father why I was doing and behaving the way I was. Living with my father - a single parent - for the better part of my formative and teenaged years, I was programmed to be a certain way as I listened to his negative comments about my mother especially on how she was the fault for all of his own ills and inability to live a good and wealthy life. *Do not get me wrong. My father was a solid and good man, flaws and all and I loved him no end as he contributed to me being who I was today. A few months before he passed, I was able to tell him how much I loved him (but that story for another day!) and everything he did for me and my brother.*

In addition, to being with my father, I attended an all-boys school. This too had not helped in my young growth, so imagine being in a home with a strong, strict male role model, then going to school to be in a classroom with just as strong, competitive classmates - both of these factors cocooned within a society of machoism and masculinity. An example of the latter, played out everyday in almost everything we see or hear around us such as music to advertising to the high incidences of domestic violence; the statistics of which, were well documented.

This revelation was like I was seeing myself for the first time, everything becoming crystal clear as if a new set of glasses had replaced my old ones - my eyes seeing ME for *ME*. I finally began to learn to love my life, each and every day and be of service to others as that, in a way, was how I was able to serve me. Trust me, it was a revelation to get to a place where one loved oneself, warts and all.

Do YOU Know How to Love YOU?

Jot down a number of ways in which you could love yourself more than you currently do. For example, like by going to the movies or shopping for nice clothes, visit a nice restaurant or travel – all by yourself. In this way you began to learn how to appreciate you and what that felt like...

How to Win?

The Mental Health Org explains that *a thorough and proper assessment is needed to ensure that there are no underlying physical causes. General practitioners are well placed to do this in the first instance so that a suitable referral to specialists can be made. This will include thorough mental-state assessment as well as physical assessment. Many physical illnesses including arthritis, diabetes, hypertension and an underactive thyroid can all cause depression. Staying and keeping active, especially taking physical exercise, can help in some cases. It is important that partners and wives are involved in engagement of the patient. Spending time with family and friends, especially if one can share one's feelings, may help.*

A balanced diet and avoiding alcohol and self-medication will also help. In mild to moderate depression, cognitive behaviour therapy has been shown to be effective. Other talking therapies may help too. However, in severe depression antidepressants may be needed. These drugs have been proven to be effective and are not addictive. The right types of medication such as a more sedating drug when the individuals are agitated and more stimulating medication when they are tired and drawn, may help.

Families should remain watchful in identifying both the symptoms and signs of suicidal ideas. Supporting and encouraging their loved ones to seek help sooner and also keeping a careful eye on the possibility of suicide, will also help. Various organisations such as the Samaritans, the Mental Health Foundation and the Royal College of Psychiatrists have information leaflets in various languages and can be downloaded easily from their respective websites. Talking about feelings is not an unmanly thing but will open up various avenues so that no one has to suffer in silence.

A 8-Step Guide to Repairing You

There was no hard and fast rule for changing what was since everybody differed as do the situations we find ourselves in. The problems may be similar but the journey and subsequent outcomes could be entirely different. What I have found going through my own trials was that it all started in one place...the only place possible. **ME**. *So what helped? What took me from where I was to where I am today?* The answers were not new, scientific or even complex.

Write

From the dawn of time and man's existence, writing has been a way of capturing thoughts and ideas. Throughout time, many books which have become the mainstay of humanness, have documented stories; such as the Bible or Koran.

To assist with healing, keep a journal. Write about the pain, experience or episode. Writing was a way of therapy, helping to expel what needed to be said. It also provided a space to reflect and to decipher

73

why we were in a particular place, and when looking back, could give a completely different perspective of that time.

Talk

I learnt this to be the basis of all the things I was supposed to do. I needed to just open up and talk about how I felt, how a situation was affecting me and recognise the consequences of my actions. This did not mean having a girlfriends-type-get-together-talking-party but just being able to say when I was hurting or dissatisfied instead of 'hiding' in fear. So, it was about finding an outlet. A sounding board. Whether that was another grounded, open and at ease male friend or friends. If it also meant seeking professional help, then so be it. There was no need to feel as if I had been persecuted, no need to allow past programming from my parents, peers or society to create negative tendencies. Sometimes this meant locking down or closing up, being aggressive or abusive when responding to situations. It was about learning and appreciating that my inner self created my outer world. And being at peace with who I was, making a more settled, rich and wealthy life.

In other words, *how important was/is the situation really? Would or will it hurt me or was it for me to listen and to learn from? How had others featured in this entire scenario? Were they coming from a place of pain or joy?*

Be Still

When the troubling waves of today, buffet and pull, tug and haul, push and grab, creating time for oneself was crucial. *Was it possible?* Yes, I say it was, because we do go to sleep, we rise (unless we were dead, of course!) and, in essence, allow time to reflect on what brought one to where one needed help with the healing. Establish a place to listen to your inner self and be aware of what *your* outer self was manifesting. I did lots of walks and meditated and the peace I found within and around, in nature, helped me to remain calm in the most trying of situations later on in my life. *How can this be done?* Turn off the TV, listen to soft music or do nothing at all - you choose. Walk to work or close your eyes while on the bus, sometimes have fun by people watching and creating the stories in your head about their own journey, maybe comparing it to yours. As weird as it seems and sounds, these all help with finding peace.

Be Thankful

Sometimes we failed to realise the smallest of what we have achieved or acquired, these were a success within itself. It could be a simple feat of getting up in the morning, inhaling and exhaling. Watch your children as they make you laugh by doing something funny. Attaining a degree, getting a job or even having your job making you redundant were all things to be grateful for; since all these things happening in your life reminded you that you were alive.

Take Responsibility

Many people would have heard this before but the thing was nobody put you in that place but **YOU**.

In my case it took a while to recognise it was my actions that took me to where I was. **ME**. I was the one responsible, nobody else, nothing else. And because of what I had created whether good or bad, things then had a way of returning to me, good or bad. Some would call it karma, others the Universe and still yet others say it was God's retribution. Whatever you may or may not call it, they all pointed to an overriding principle that would continue through the eons of time.

Dream of a Better Tomorrow

Tomorrow was always a better day. I found out through my journey that as long as I was alive, my living in the present was all that mattered.

Read Uplifting and Empowering Books

Prior to venturing into my wilderness, the lady I was going out with at the time gave me a present for my birthday which became my 'bible', in a way. The book, *Spirit of A Man* by Iyanla Vanzant. I found it to be the greatest and most important read for me.

Helping to plant a seed for change and growth, at a time when I was at my lowest ebb, I occupied a beautiful bookstore known as Knowledge Bookstore, Brampton. The store became my sanctuary, a place where I escaped and buried myself in the Black books there. Books about me, books about Our Ancestors and *their* struggle, books on how to get to where I wanted to be from where I was - phenomenal and wonderful books. Great and inspiring books[8]. By reading, I clawed myself away from the abyss that was expecting me to sink into its blackness.

Be Around Good People

There was something else I learned whilst being in a negative state - you could never get enough good people around you. People who loved you when you were at your worst or even your best; people who accepted you for you, warts and all; without inhibitions or judgment; people who told you

---

[8] Just a couple: Susan Jeffers: *Feel the Fear and Do It Anyway,* Jack Canfield and Janet Switzer: *The Success Principles: how to get from where you are to where you want to be*

the truth even when it did not fit within your psyche or was not good to hear. Those were and still were the tools to my basic way of living nowadays and with their help, I approached life with a different perspective.

Patience

Again, my solutions may not be for everyone as we were all in different places in our life journey. What took me fits and starts, and years to recognise and accept may take another more or less time. I would also say that one of the greatest achievements to grow from the experience was just to be patient. Take time with yourself. As humans, we were made to make mistakes and as such would encounter potholes, bumps and humps. The thing was not to be derailed by the experience or even the outcome and progress as slowly as we can, learning from the lessons.

Forgiveness

Importantly, and above all else, learn to forgive yourself. Leading on from patience, forgiveness was one of the biggest healers I would suggest. It helped to recognise that any pain began with you and as such, only you could heal yourself; regardless of what others may or may not have done to you, including parents, friends, family, teachers, boss etc. You had the power to overcome. To stop the cycle. To mend the hurt. To embrace and appreciate the hurt. Forgiveness was a must.

Final Word

Note, what I have shared in this book was my personal journey. Our Ancestors were kidnapped and brought to what was called the *New World* centuries ago – as such, so much change occurred within us as African people: physically, mentally, emotionally and spiritually. Thus, uplifted from our natural habitat and taken into new environments we lost a lot, including sacred traditions and even our names. We were also subjected to horrors that we still felt today, like being closed and uncommunicative (and there were reasons for that), being one of them. But importantly, and over generations, we were still able to keep remnants such as guiding our young from a child and into an adult and this, sometimes, more by trial and error. And yet, those major bits of being able to openly communicate, be confident in and understanding self, appreciative of responsibility, being a rounded adult and being a wholesome parent, community cohesion and so on; were now being defined within a new paradigm. Thus as African or Black men we were already starting at a deficit and...*yet...and this was where everyone could relate, regardless of who they were or where they came from...*

This paradigm or standard affected each and every one of us since it now consisted of a *modern* "rat race" way of working with *modern* technology heavily influencing how we lived, leading to a now so-called *modern* lifestyle. From communicating with each other to how we built relationships, the impact of work-life balance plus so much more; has created its own pressures and these have moved us away from the core of who we were as human beings, forcing us to live in a constructed, yet false reality. It was within this "reality" where we tried to hold onto who we really were, resulting in an internal struggle that drove us into places we never knew existed. I experienced that.

It was my sincere hope that this book assisted you or someone you knew in navigating this experience that affected so many of us - men as well as women. Yet, I do hope that more of us *men*, in particular, began the dialogue in how we could support each other in facing this silent killer.

Written in love.

Kwame MA McPherson

An Overcoming Depression Checklist

Note, what I have shared in this book was my personal journey. Thus, I am no counsellor or psychologist and everything I have stated within this book is based on my own experience. This checklist was just a jump-start for you and for further empowerment, I would recommend professional assistance to support you in your journey.

List a time when you had a good or bad experience? ☐

Identify what caused you to be where you are? ☐

Can you recall the times when *you* selected the 'wrong' people? ☐

Who are YOU? ☐

What are YOU doing and why? ☐

Who brought YOU here? ☐

Do YOU know how to love YOU? ☐

Where I Am Today

The time I went through my dark moment was well and truly behind me, and since that episode, I am much stronger, phenomenally patient, having a greater appreciation for life and all that it brought.

I could have never have made it without our Creator, Ancestors, partners, friends and family all showing me the path I needed to follow. And since those heady days, I have been showered with so much opportunity and blessing, that it could only be a reflection of where I was internally. There have been so many others that my life-purpose has assisted. Many who have gone to share their own life purpose, changing so many more lives. I have written and continue to write and publish articles, novellas and novels. I have been able to visit to Amsterdam and meet with a billionaire and millionaires, negotiating with them to bring a new business concept to a virgin country; I have travelled to Hamburg (that experience featured in *7 Tips for the Virgin Entrepreneur: doing it for the first time*), been able to obtain another unique and ground-breaking idea, again into a new market. I learnt so much, enjoying the experiences and visualising more of the same. So much more has happened with me, professionally and entrepreneurship-wise but, even though it has not been all sunshine and sunflowers, I was at peace with everything. Even with the finding of the eventual "imperfect perfect" partner, that was okay too as we sought to be together mentally, emotionally, physically and spiritually. For now, I was so grateful with what I have been through and seen within such an incredible journey.

Reaching here to share the trauma as well as the joys of such a life, I was thankful. When I was going through my low time, there were those who believed in me when I had not and to them, I was eternally thankful. They contributed to the service I now give to others.

Roll-on the next chapter in my life...

About Cape Coast Castle

This castle in Cape Coast, Ghana—once known as the Gold Coast of West Africa—was one of around 40 "slave castles" that served as prisons and embarkation points for slaves en route to the Americas (the Caribbean, South America, and the U.S.). Thousands of enslaved Africans from regions near and far, sometimes hundreds of miles away, were taken to these castles to be sold to slave ships. One of the most well-known parts of Cape Coast Castle, that you can visit today, is the "Door of No Return," which led slaves out of the castle and onto the ships setting off on the Middle Passage. Their boat journeys could last several months, and an estimated 15 percent of slaves died aboard, en route. Somewhere around 12 million slaves were sent from Africa, millions of whom died in the process. Cape Coast Castle was a way station in history's largest, and darkest, forced human migration. **Source:** https://www.atlasobscura.com/places/cape-coast-castle

Check out my blog:

https://whywemendonttalk.blogspot.com

Additional Resources and Contacts
(Not an exhaustive list)

Jamaica

Jamaica Mental Health Advocacy Network
https://dogoodjamaica.org/organizations/jamaica_mental_health_advocacy_network/
Ministry of Health https://www.moh.gov.jm/divisions-agencies/divisions/mental-health-unit/

United Kingdom

Mental health charities, groups and services

Mental Health Foundation	020 7803 1101	Improving the lives of those with mental health problems or learning difficulties.
Together	020 7780 7300	Supports people through mental health services.
The Centre for Mental Health	020 7827 8300	Working to improve the quality of life for people with mental health problems.
Depression Alliance	0845 123 2320	Provides information and support to those who are affected by depression via publications, supporter services and a network of self-help groups.
BACP Find a Therapist Directory	01455 883300	Through the British Association for Counselling & Psychotherapy (BACP) you can find out more about counselling services in your area.
PANDAS Foundation	0843 28 98 401 (every day from 9am-8pm)	PANDAS Foundation vision is to support every individual with pre (antenatal), postnatal depression or postnatal psychosis in England, Wales and Scotland. We campaign to raise awareness and remove the stigma. We provide our PANDAS Help Line, Support Groups offer online advice to all and much more.

General advice and support

<u>Citizens Advice</u>		Gives free confidential information and advice to help people sort out their money, legal, consumer and other problems. Support for children and young people
<u>Young Minds</u>	020 7336 8445	Provides information and advice for anyone with concerns about the mental health of a child or young person.
<u>Childline</u>	0800 1111	Free, national helpline for children and young people in trouble or danger.
<u>Nightline</u>		Listening, support and information service run by students for students. Other places you could go for support
<u>Age Concern</u>	0800 009966	Infoline on issues relating to older people.
<u>Lesbian and Gay Switchboard</u>	020 7837 7324	Provides information, support and referral services.
<u>Refugee Council</u>	020 7346 6700	The UK's largest organisation working with refugees and asylum seekers.
<u>Relate</u>	0300 100 1234	Offers advice, relationship counselling, sex therapy, workshops, mediation, consultations and support.
<u>Education Support Partnership</u>	08000 562 561	A 24/7 telephone support line which gives teachers access to professional coaches and counsellors 365 days a year. The network also campaigns for change within schools and education policy in order to improve the wellbeing, mental and physical health of teachers.
<u>Anxiety UK</u>	08444 775 774	Works to relieve and support those living with anxiety disorders by providing information, support and understanding via an extensive range of services, including 1:1 therapy.

Carers organisations

<u>Carers UK</u>		Carers UK is the voice of carers. It improves their lives by providing information, advice, support and by

campaigning for change.

United States of America

(Not an exhaustive list as each state has its own provision)

Mental Health.gov https://www.mentalhealth.gov/

Mental Health http://www.mentalhealthamerica.net/finding-therapy

Healthy Place https://www.healthyplace.com/other-info/mental-illness-overview/free-mental-health-services-and-how-to-find-them

NOTES

NOTES

NOTES